the pulbrook and gould book of flower arrangement

the
pulbrook and gould

photographs by michael plomer

book of
flower arrangement

edited by frances ann hawkes

 barrie and jenkins

First published by Barrie & Rockliff, The Cresset Press
Text set by Yendall & Company Ltd., London
Colour origination by Supreme Litho Limited, London
Printed in the Netherlands by Drukkerij de Lange van Leer N.V.

First published 1968
Reprinted 1970, 1972
Reprinted in 1978 by
Barrie & Jenkins Limited
24 Highbury Crescent, London N5 1RX

ISBN 0 214 66728 6

Many people, in many different ways, have helped to write this book. It
would be difficult to acknowledge each contribution in detail, but the
author wishes to express profound thanks to everyone who allowed cameras
and lights to invade their houses, or patiently answered questions, or worked
unreasonable hours without complaint.

The quotation on page 14 is from Osbert Lancaster's Here of all Places *and
appears by kind permission of the author and Publishers, John Murray Limited.*

F. A. H.

contents

historical background

The earliest examples of floral decoration date from the development of domestic and agricultural civilisations. Wall-paintings and relief sculptures found in the Nile Valley (which had been under cultivation for several thousand years) show that cut flowers were arranged in bowls and vases for decoration. Many vases have been excavated from Ancient Egyptian tombs; they were made in a variety of materials such as crude glass, precious metals and decorated faience. The flower used most was the lotus blossom (Egyptian water-lily), a symbol of the goddess Isis whom the ancient Egyptians believed had taught their ancestors to cultivate wheat and barley, so changing them from barbarians to a civilised people.

In the ancient civilisations of Greece, Persia and Rome (as well as Egypt) it was customary to deck sacrificial victims and corpses with garlands of flowers; but finally any festive occasion became an excuse to wear flowers, and for the first time they were a commercial proposition. Soon professional growers were cultivating flower gardens to supply the professional 'florists' with material for their wreaths and garlands. Darius, the great Persian king (d.486 B.C.), is said to have had nearly fifty professional wreath- and garland-makers attached to his household. In decadent Rome the rose (discovered in the fourth century B.C. by the Egyptians), became the most fashionable flower. The petals were scattered on the streets, and the blossoms hung in festoons around statues and pillars, or used in great profusion to adorn banqueting tables and couches during festivities. Eventually the demand for roses became so great that the plants had to be imported and forced into bloom near the hot-water system.

We know something of the varieties of flowers, foliage and herbs available to the Greeks and Romans from mummified mortuary garlands, perfume recipes and, of course, their literature. Apart from roses, they cultivated cornflowers, irises, peonies, poppies, lilies and violets, and ivy, laurel, mint and thyme, amongst others. Roman women used herbs to freshen and scent their houses and clothes – a custom which spread throughout western Europe with the Roman conquests. It was the Romans, too, who introduced horticulture to Britain, where there is today perhaps a more passionate and universal interest in the subject than anywhere else in the West. However, although the Romans were gardeners and florists, they rarely arranged cut flowers in vases; while the ancient Greeks, who made countless beautiful vases and urns, did not intend that they should hold flowers. Indeed, it was not until the Renaissance that the practice of keeping cut flowers in the house developed in the West.

From the decline and fall of the Roman Empire and through the Dark Ages (roughly from the death of the Emperor Constantine in 337 A.D. until the 1000's) civilisation in Western Europe went into an eclipse. The West Roman Empire collapsed under the burden of a vastly increased army and civil service and extreme disorder and poverty resulted, while their hard-won territories were looted and laid waste by invading barbarians: Goths, Huns and Vandals. In an atmosphere of unrest and economic depression, people quickly abandoned or forgot the arts and crafts which they had learned and developed in a more peaceful era. This was not true of the Byzantine Empire, where much of Greek and Roman culture was preserved, nor of the Arab sphere which extended to Spain and North Africa. However, in the greater part of Western Europe it was not in effect until the early Middle Ages that the arts – and horticulture – began to revive.

During the Middle Ages, horticulture – for pleasure and study as well as profit – became one of the many fields in which the Church took an active interest. As the great landowner of the period, it is not surprising that the Church should devote some of its time and energies to cultivation: most monasteries had large kitchen gardens, orchards, sometimes flower gardens, and of course their own livestock. They grew all their own vegetables, selling the surplus locally, and an enormous variety of herbs from which they produced medicines. Flowers were also used for medicinal purposes, but their beauty must have inspired many of the designs created by the monks for their illuminated manuscripts – though the flowers represented were so stylised as to be frequently unrecognisable.

Pagan tradition was so strong in the Middle Ages that the Church had found it politic to incorporate many barely-disguised ancient rites in the new religious order. Flowers had been much used on festive occasions in pre-Christian times, and so it came about that the priests of St. Paul's, London, were still wearing flower crowns (*coronae sacerdotales*) in processions in the 13th century. It is also probable that cut flowers were used then as now to decorate church interiors on feast days. Henry VI of England designated some land for the expressed purpose of planting trees and flowers for the service of the church.

The Crusaders developed an interest in plants and flowers during their extensive travels and even succeeded, in the face of tremendous odds, in bringing home some of the strange and exotic specimens they had found. But at home flowers were still regarded in the light of religious symbolism: containers holding cut flowers – particularly the white *Lilium candidum* (symbolising both fertility and chastity) – appear in many Annunciation paintings of the period; and, because of their religious connotations, it was considered disrespectful, even sacrilegious, to arrange cut flowers for the house. (Even today many people believe it 'unlucky' to bring certain flowers indoors, little realising that they are perpetuating ancient religious tabus. An example of this is the superstition attached to may [hawthorn blossom], which once symbolised the crown of thorns.)

With the Renaissance in the 15th century came a decline in the absolute power of the Church and a new sense of freedom for the individual. It was a time of exploration and scientific discovery, of a revival of letters and the arts; now, at last, flower decoration began a slow, but this time continuous, development in Western Europe. At first the interest in flowers was academic rather than aesthetic, but beside the new intellectual curiosity grew an appreciation of beauty.

Like England at this time, Holland was a great maritime power with many colonies in exotic places, and the Dutch botanists quickly took advantage of the situation. Soon they were far ahead of their contemporaries in other lands. Carolus Clusius, an eminent 16th century Flemish botanist and professor at Leyden, collected rare plants which he acquired by corresponding with foreign botanists and by encouraging ambassadors, merchants and friends to bring him specimens from abroad. Illustrated works were published on his findings, along with those of many other distinguished botanists such as Leonard Fuchs and Dodonaeus. They were fortunate in that the invention of moveable type in the 1440's and the increased efficiency of book production during the 16th century (especially the use of engraved plates for illustrations instead of wood blocks) had made it possible to render detail with greater clarity and precision. The dissemination of information on horticulture soon created its own demand. Rich patrons commissioned books with elaborate illustrations; these were not confined to technical diagrams of horticultural specimens, but also showed flowers purely for their beauty.

The awakening interest in flowers for their own sake very naturally led to a fashion for gardening, of which one of the best known aspects is the tulip craze, which began in Holland in the 1560's. One of Clusius'

correspondents was Busbecq, ambassador of the Emperor Ferdinand I to the court of Sultan Soliman in Turkey. He had been impressed by the tulips he saw growing in Turkish gardens and sent some seed to Clusius, who began to produce bulbs. Mutations in colour were soon achieved, interest grew, and quite suddenly tulip-growing became a national pastime. The excitement generated by the unpredictable variations in colour (now known to be caused by a virus) gave rise to an inflationary trade in tulip bulbs: rich competitors are known to have paid literally hundreds of pounds for a single one.

Flower arrangement received curious treatment at the hands of the Dutch during the late 16th and 17th centuries: it became fashionable to brighten rooms with floral paintings, rather than with vases of real flowers. Still-life or flower-piece painting as a style spread through Holland in the wake of the Reformation. The Protestant Church did not believe in commissioning paintings, and the still-life, hitherto a minor part of the composition of religious paintings – included for its symbolism – developed independently. This did not mean that flowers instantly lost their symbolic significance: the sacred element was merely overlaid by a humanistic approach.

The disintegration of feudal rigidity and the rise of the bourgeoisie to positions of wealth and power during the protestant Reformation had direct bearing on the development of flower-piece painting into a fashionable art form. The 17th century Dutch burghers and merchants were to all intents and purposes the ruling class, because they controlled the economy in a commercially orientated country. As such, they assumed the role of dictators of taste and patrons of the arts, a role that had belonged exclusively to the Roman Catholic Church. The breakdown of the Church's domination of cultural life and the change from a God-centred to a self-centred view of cosmic order gave rise to more self-indulgence and love of luxury than men had previously permitted themselves. A natural outgrowth of this *nouveau riche* materialist culture was a general enthusiasm for domestic interior decoration, and this was the heyday of flower-piece painting in Holland.

An important factor in the development of the art was undoubtedly the climate. As Hermine van Guldener points out in her book *The Flower-piece in Painting*, Holland has a cold damp climate, and in winter it is often dark and gloomy; under such conditions people are bound to spend the greater part of their time indoors, and will make a correspondingly greater effort to ensure that their houses are attractive and comfortable. Flower-piece paintings were certain to be popular for their brilliant colours, beautiful design and the outdoor element they brought into potentially grim Dutch interiors. But why the choice should have fallen on painted flowers rather than real ones is a matter for speculation. Possibly the main reason was that paintings have traditionally been coveted as status symbols.

From the middle of the 17th century until the first decades of the 18th century the popularity of flower-piece painting spread far and wide. Pictures were much in demand in the courts of Europe and the Dutch artists never lacked commissions. The paintings of this period reflected the growing prosperity of the middle classes in their increased gaiety, richness and exuberant sensuality. Full-blown roses, enormous peonies and ripe fruit displayed in rich vases of silver, glass and porcelain, dominated the compositions.

In attempting to trace the history of flower arrangement, a useful guide is the development of containers specially designed to hold cut flowers. Although, as we have seen, certain ancient civilisations produced vases, in Europe they were virtually unknown before the 14th century. Until that time, we can assume that ordinary household vessels such as bottles, jugs, ewers and bowls were used, on the fairly infrequent occasions when flowers were brought into the house. Some 15th century Italian paintings show flowers arranged in decorative vessels of Venetian glass and Italian majolica, but it should be remembered that Italian civilisation was far in advance of the rest of Western Europe at this time. The Italian trade factor was also important: it was the Venetian merchants who had introduced Chinese ceramics to Europe. The ceramic trade subsequently flourished all over Europe, but more especially in England and the Netherlands after the founding of the East India Companies (England in 1600, Holland in 1602).

Blue and white Chinese porcelain became extremely popular, and Dutch craftsmen quickly learnt to imitate the style comparatively cheaply. Their blue and white ceramics were in fact faience pottery, not porcelain, and were called after their place of manufacture, Delft (the industry had been moved from Haarlem to Delft towards the end of the 16th century). This industry reached its peak in the second half of the 17th century, but collapsed during the French occupation of Holland at the end of the 18th century.

In 17th century England imitations of Chinese, Italian, Hispano-Mauresque majolica and pottery, and 'Persian Blue' Nevers ware were being produced in considerable quantities. Deltfware, too, was much in demand and English Delft was manufactured in Bristol, Brislington, Wincanton, Dublin and probably Glasgow. By the 18th century Liverpool had become a centre of the industry and was exporting large quantities to America, where for the first time people had the leisure to cultivate sophisticated hobbies.

Trade with the Orient obviously did much to stimulate interest in flower arrangement in Europe. Not only did new varieties of plants and ceramics become known to Europeans, they also had the opportunity to learn of a creed and way of life which differed much from their own. In China the art of flower arranging had become an integral part of daily life through its close association with Buddhism and the teachings of Confucius (651–479 B.C.). The Chinese style was, and is, characterised by extreme simplicity and asceticism, based on the Confucian precepts that (1) beauty in large quantities is distracting and spiritually indigestible, therefore real enjoyment only comes from the ability to apprehend an object completely; and that (2) a single flower is a perfect microcosm of the whole cycle of life, and therefore sufficient material for contemplation. The tendency towards stark simplicity was further supported by the Buddhist belief that all life is precious and must be preserved. Any Chinese flower arrangement which takes the form of a massed bouquet is a direct result of Western influence, and could not have existed before the 17th century.

As the approach to flower arrangement in China was governed by religious and intellectual convictions, the end-product was necessarily imbued with a precise significance. Every flower had a meaning and every important event in life was associated with a particular flower. Each season, to take but one example, was represented by a flower: autumn by a chrysanthemum, winter by white plum blossom, spring by a peony, and summer by a lotus blossom. The idea of longevity, sacred to Buddhism, was also of central importance and was referred to in all arrangements. The Chinese countryside was rich in its variety of flowers, trees and plants which, together with the extraordinary landscape, undoubtedly fostered a national fascination with Nature and the natural sciences.

In Western culture materialism has run rife since the Renaissance, producing a very different art, characterised by frivolity, extravagance and artifice. Difference in outlook did not, however, prevent European merchants and travellers from appreciating Chinese art and horticultural techniques to the full. The Chinese were highly skilled gardeners, experienced in the cultivation of many plants, as well as being far ahead of Europe in botanical research (they had a system for the classification of medicinal herbs and drugs as early as the Han period [207 B.C. – 220 A.D.] and had catalogued some thirty-five species of chrysanthemum by the 11th century). When the European explorers returned, they brought with them not only new horticultural techniques, but the concept of flower arranging as an art, which they developed in their own way, discarding the irrelevant religious element.

The 16th and 17th centuries saw a quickening interest in horticulture in England as well as on the Continent, encouraged by a similar expansion in trade. During the reign of Elizabeth I, thanks to the activities of Her Majesty's large merchant navy, the general boom in commerce, and the influx of Protestant refugees escaping Spanish persecution, many new flowers were brought to England. Among the plants introduced at that time are many which are now particularly associated with English gardens: daffodils, narcissi, laburnum, lilac, lobelia, pinks, tulips and auricula.

Until Tudor times it had been customary to strew floors with rushes, for warmth and easy disposal of refuse (which was swept out periodically with the rushes). Herbs were scattered on the rushes to alleviate the stench and in an attempt to prevent diseases, such as the bubonic plague. The Elizabethans introduced a refinement by mixing flowers with the rushes, a custom that persisted to the end of the 17th century. They also used to put 'posies' or 'nosegays' in living rooms and bed-chambers – but again, this custom was for health rather than decorative purposes, since the perfume of flowers, as well as herbs, was believed to be beneficial. Fresh air was considered harmful, if not fatal to the sick, and the windows and doors were tightly closed, so that the resulting atmosphere was quite overpowering and can have done little to help the patient. (In France, Henry III [1574–1589], who was addicted to strong perfumes, had the Royal bedchamber strewn with fresh flowers, and petals every morning for the *lever*: the combined effect of a roaring fire and the heavy scent of flowers occasionally caused some unfortunate Gentlemen of the Bedchamber and other assembled courtiers to faint.)

Until the 17th century, English flower arranging could at the most be regarded as a folk art: the approach was spontaneous, individual and completely lacking in formality. With the spread of gardening techniques and the profusion of flowers and plants available to everyone, people began to appreciate that flowers could be a cheap but highly effective form of interior decoration. By the 18th century, books on horticulture were appearing which differed from earlier works on the subject in that they included helpful suggestions on combining flowers for arrangements. Julia Berrall quotes from Philip Miller's *The Gardener's Dictionary* (published in London c.1731–1739) a receipt for an arrangement of monkshood 'cultivated for the beauty of its long spikes of blue flowers' and guelder roses, recommending that they be attractively arranged together 'to adorn halls and other apartments'.

From the end of the 17th century, ornamental vases were produced in quantities in Britain. The Chelsea factory even went so far as to produce ceramic flowers with ormolu stems to be used for arrangements when fresh material was unavailable. During the Georgian era, classical designs for flower containers were favoured, particularly the urn. The most famous of these were made by Josiah Wedgwood, who created simulated porphyry and perfected processes for reproducing an antique effect. He designed vases to conform to his principles of flower arrangement, set forth in a pamphlet entitled 'The Art of Disposing the Most Beautiful Products of Nature'.

In England, the fashion for formal gardens in the Dutch and French manner declined towards the middle of the 18th century. Allées, parterres, terraces, neatly trimmed hedges, gave place to 'wild' gardens. The eye had finally grown weary of the elaborate topiary art (the training and severe pruning of trees and shrubs into geometrical and animal shapes) which had been practised *ad nauseam* throughout the country, even occasionally in cottage gardens. The revolt, encouraged by oriental influence, was led and shaped by three great figures: William Kent (c.1685–1748), Sir William Chambers (1723–96) and Lancelot 'Capability' Brown (1715–83).

Kent, an architect in the Palladian style, used to landscape the gardens around the house he had designed, making full use of the natural topography. Chambers, also an architect, first gained attention by designing the ornamental buildings at Kew. He had lived in China, and designed a garden in the Chinese

manner. The first of its kind in England, it was laid out in curves rather than straight lines, with unclipped trees judiciously placed for a natural effect. But the height of perfection in landscape gardening was attained by Capability Brown (so nicknamed through telling his clients that their estates had 'great capabilities'). His work achieved immediately popularity, and he was appointed Royal Gardener at Hampton Court. He is still admired today by architects and gardeners as the greatest genius in his field.

At this period interest in flower gardens all but disappeared, as they did not have a place in naturalistic garden design. Flowers for the house were reduced to a functional status and banished to the kitchen garden, while more delicate plants were grown in hothouses and conservatories. They were looked upon as minor embellishments: small bunches were used to decorate drawing rooms elegantly furnished by Sheraton, Hepplewhite and Chippendale; women wore tiny bouquets at the throat, in their hair, and carried them in baskets as accessories. Although there are few contemporary pictorial records of flower arrangements, it can be surmised that the style corresponded to the style of gardening, and that arrangements were therefore loosely composed in a way which would appear natural and graceful. Artificiality and extreme stylisation are the legacy of the Victorians and will be discussed below.

It was during the 18th century that interest in flower arrangement was first expressed in America. Especially in the northern parts of the colonies, the early settlers' time had been fully occupied by the struggle for survival in a harsh climate and under constant threat of Red Indian attack. The puritan colonists' gardens were strictly utilitarian, producing either nourishment or medicine. Some flowers were grown, but only because they were used in herbal remedies: roses could be made into a syrup for sore throats, a mild anaesthetic or a purge; peonies were believed to have healing properties and were probably rendered into an ointment for burns and wounds. Many of the flowers and plants cultivated had been grown from seeds and bulbs which the colonists had brought with them.

Farther south, in New Amsterdam, settled by the Dutch in 1626, life was less perilous than in the Massachusetts Bay colonies, and there was more opportunity for pleasurable pursuits. As the way of life in any colony reflects that of the country of origin, it was inevitable that the Dutch settlers should be keen and clever gardeners. They made excellent orchards of apple, pear, plum, peach, fig and cherry trees, and cultivated many of the flowers that were currently popular in Holland: gillyflowers, guelder roses, marigolds, violets and, of course, tulips. They also attempted simple flower arrangements, using common household vessels. When the English took over the settlement in 1664, the ground was, so to speak, well prepared.

In the southern colonies of Virginia, the settlers were more closely linked with England than the New England renegades. In 1698 Williamsburg was founded as the capital city, becoming the centre of society and providing an atmosphere which bred sophisticated culture. The colony rapidly grew rich and leisured through commerce and the introduction of slave labour. Wealthy men imported fine English furniture, textiles and china for their large neo-classical wooden houses. Ambitious to emulate the grandeur and elegance of their English counterparts, they also imported many varieties of plants and trees from Europe and laid out exotic gardens which flourished in the humid, semi-tropical climate. Naturalists and botanists were fascinated to discover the indigenous varieties of plants, and a lively exchange grew up between them and English gentlemen gardeners. Naturally the mortality rate of botanical specimens making the transatlantic crossing was extremely high, but this apparently did not deter the enthusiastic correspondents.

When gardening was established as a proper patrician occupation, interest in flower arranging developed. Native wild flowers and grasses were used, as well as garden flowers; the custom of gathering material during the summer months to be dried and used in winter decorations probably evolved during this period. Corn cobs, cattails, sea lavender and straw flowers were popular for use in dry arrangements, and still are today, particularly for the table centre-piece at the feast of Thanksgiving.

Few vases appeared in America until the 18th century, when they began to arrive from England and China. All fine ceramics of that period were imported, because it was not until the last decades of the century that American craftsmen had begun to achieve standards of design and craftsmanship equal to their European counterparts. The vogue for *Chinoiseries* was never so strong in the colonies as in England, since the colonists preferred a more classical style in architecture, furniture and gardens (Georgian neo-classicism persisted through the Federal period and the early days of the Republic until roughly 1830). However, Chinese ceramics were sought after by some colonial gentlemen, and vases, sets of dishes and other ceramic objects were specially commissioned from China – many of them decorated with American emblems such as the eagle and stars. Unfortunately no real records exist of flower arrangements of this period: the containers are all that remain. It can only be surmised that they were similar to English and French arrangements of the same period, though perhaps less sophisticated and elaborate, in keeping with colonial adaptation of English and Continental decorative styles and fashions generally.

The evolution of flower decoration in France followed a very different pattern from that in Holland, England and Colonial America. Flower motifs had been extensively used since the Middle Ages in tapestries and in the massive woodcarvings which adorned grand interiors (such as at Fontainebleau) and, until the late 18th century, the French preferred flowers in this form, or in flower-piece painting in the Dutch manner, to fresh arrangements.

All the decorative arts thrived under royal patronage, particularly during the wildly extravagant days of Louis XIV's reign, when the best artists and craftsmen of the time were employed at Versailles. André Le Nôtre, the master landscape artist of this period, was responsible for planning not only the famous park for the Château de Versailles but also those of Chantilly, Vaux and Dijon. His work, always on a vast scale, is distinguished by symmetry and the use of geometrical shapes, with formal parterres and long allées of severely clipped trees and hedges. Orange trees, which had become fashionable, were cultivated in the famous *orangerie* at Versailles. They were placed in marble urns and silver tubs and were the most usual form of decoration for state apartments and the vast *galerie des glaces*. In such impressive surroundings an arrangement of cut flowers would have been so insignificant as to be pointless; however, flowers were grown in the kitchen gardens and were probably used for table decoration.

Louis XIV had created Versailles to be the centre of court life and in order to keep an eye on the aristocracy. A summons to Versailles could only be ignored at the risk of incurring the King's intense displeasure (which could mean life exile, confiscation of lands, and the disinheriting of the victim's family). Once installed at Versailles, in appallingly cramped and uncomfortable quarters, the nobles would be haunted by the fear of committing some small faux-pas which could lead to rustication. The disgrace attached to rustication was such that suicide was sometimes considered a reasonable alternative. So unnatural an environment soon had its effect on the unfortunate aristocracy: they became a society of idle pleasure-seekers and intriguers, frivolous, effeminate, lacking in integrity, and with ludicrously expensive tastes. It was not surprising under these conditions that women should become the dictators of taste and arbiters of fashion, and during the subsequent reign, that of Louis XV, the King's mistress, Madame de Pompadour, was to have lasting influence on the arts.

Antoinette Poisson, Marquise de Pompadour, of bourgeois origin, had a passionate and intelligent interest in the arts. Her influence over the king was so great that she was Queen in all but name during the years when she was Louis XV's titular mistress (1745–64). Her excursions into politics were frequently misguided, but her dedicated and generous protection and encouragement of artisans, painters and men of letters can only be considered to have been beneficial to the arts (while costing the State vast sums of money which it could ill afford). The craze for *Chinoiseries* that obsessed connoisseurs and collectors at this period was directly due to Madame de Pompadour. She was particularly interested in china-ware, and was responsible for obtaining large royal subsidies for the Sèvres factory, which subsequently produced quantities of decorative porcelain, including vases in brilliant colours, hand-painted with scenes and floral patterns. These were made in many different sizes and shapes: bowls in the Chinese style, épergnes and urns. Other vases of the period were made in crystal, marble and metals.

The style of this era, in contrast to the formality and ponderous grandeur of Louis XIV's reign, was characterised by lightness and grace with a touch of the frivolous, exotic and amorous. The label given to the period, with particular reference to architecture and furniture, is rococo (probably a fanciful derivation from the French *rocaille* – pebble work), and usually refers to an abundance of conventional shell- and scroll-work and meaningless decoration. The term was later used to describe anything which was tastelessly florid and ornate. Harmonious colour schemes were preferred to dramatic contrasts, and flowers in pale, refined colours were used in combination with yellow.

The rococo style remained popular until Marie-Antoinette came to power with Louis XVI in 1774. Her Austrian upbringing had given her simpler tastes than her unfriendly subjects at the French court, and she had a love of nature that they lacked, which led her to popularise the philosophy of Jean-Jacques Rousseau.

From the end of Louis XIV's reign, cultural activity had retreated gradually from the court to the more intimate atmosphere of the homes of socialites and the intelligentsia. A corresponding interest in domestic interior decoration developed, and with it a vogue for small flower decorations in the bouquet style. This fashion was particularly favoured in the days of Madame de Pompadour, but continued in a less stylised form until the Revolution began in 1789. After Napoleon's coronation as Emperor in 1804 there was a rapid return to formality and severity in decorative styles – following the new masculine and military court fashions – in strong contrast to the delicate, feminine character of Louis XV and XVI furnishings. Quite understandably flowers went out of fashion as decorative motifs and were superseded by symbols of victory such as the sphinx (commemorating Napoleon's Egyptian campaign), the lion, laurel wreaths and golden bees. It was an age of neo-classicism: the official architects, Percier and Fontaine, took their inspiration from the architecture of ancient Rome, and much decoration was inspired by the discovery of the art of ancient Egypt, which tends to be pompous, domineering and ceremonial in character. Classical fruits were used for decorations in place of flowers: pomegranates, quinces, grapes, figs, were arranged in bowls of Grecian or Roman design, alabaster urns and cornucopias.

The private botanical garden, popular in Marie-Antoinette's time, was increasingly becoming a fashionable interest for high society. The Empress Josephine had a beautiful, semi-landscaped garden at her retreat, Malmaison, on the outskirts of Paris. She was particularly interested in rose-growing; her roses were portrayed by the official artist, Redoute, in several hundred paintings.

The Victorian Age in England lasted for nearly three-quarters of the 19th century (1837–1901), embracing a number of different styles and social attitudes. The period can be roughly divided into three sections, Early, Middle and Late Victorian, and it is to the styles prevalent during the last two sections that people usually refer when discussing 'Victorian' taste and fashion. For the first time the middle-classes were comparatively prosperous, and better educated than ever before. The Queen had made respectability and happy family life fashionable, and it was therefore natural that all forms of domestic art and architecture should receive a good deal of attention.

Victoria always favoured dark colours and sober styles, but after the death of Prince Albert she went into permanent mourning, and the country followed suit to a certain degree. The popular colours for dress and furnishings were dark crimson, mulberry, mustard, magenta, purple, royal blue and brown. Furniture tended to be heavy and ornate and made of dark woods such as mahogany and rosewood. Plants and flowers became extremely popular for interior decoration, but were chosen usually for their stiffness or toning colours. This was the heyday of potted plants: the aspidistra and the rubber plant (*ficus elastica*), cinerarias, *coleus*, and discreet or formal flowers like pansies and tulips. There was also an influx of imported plants, among which were camellias, tree peonies, *gladioli* and nasturtiums. Dahlias became increasingly popular because they were good hybridizers and a wide range of colours could be easily produced.

The Victorians were also responsible for a romantic flower symbolism, in which practically every known flower, plant or even tree was endowed with sentimental significance or an edifying property. The language of flowers became universally accepted and understood, to the point where messages could be delivered in the form of a bouquet. For instance, a combination of monkshood, mountain ash and blue violet meant: Danger is near. Be prudent, be faithful. Roses stood for beauty, bluebells for constancy, peonies for shame, columbine for folly, pansies (*pensées*) for thoughts, cyclamen for riches, and so on – the list was exhaustive.

There is no question that interest in horticulture and flower arranging reached a peak at this period. Arrangements were considered not only an aesthetic contribution to the domestic environment, but the process of arranging flowers was believed to be morally edifying – a consideration of prime importance to any right-thinking Victorian. On this subject, Julia Berrall quotes from *Godey's Lady's Book* (the contemporary equivalent of our popular women's weekly magazines): 'They [flowers] employ the hand, delight the eye and inform and edify the mind, and unlike many artificial objects, the enjoyment and instruction they afford are within the reach of all, the poor may partake as well as the rich.' Mrs Beeton's *Book of Household Management*, the most famous domestic treatise ever written, also comments on the growing fashion for flower arrangement and stresses its value as an occupation for women of taste and intelligence: 'The decoration of tables at the present time is almost universal, and so does the taste for it grow and develop, that what was formerly left in the hands of the head servants in large establishments, who had no difficulty in packing the heavy épergnes with fruit or flowers, now forms a wide field of labour for artistic taste and skill. Hostesses in the season vie with each other as to whose table shall be the most elegant, and often spend almost as much upon the flowers as upon the dinner itself, employing for the floral arrangement people who make a profession of this pleasant occupation. Home decoration is practised by those who have the time, and we can imagine no household duty more attractive to the ladies of the house than that of making their tables beautiful with the exquisite floral produce of the different seasons, exercising their taste in devising new ways for employing the materials at their command. Young people should have the taste for arranging flowers encouraged, and be allowed to assist in decorating the table. Care should be taken not to overload the table with flowers.'

Victorian flower arrangements generally had a rigid, symmetrical shape, usually triangular or circular, and the flowers were almost always wired. A typical example of this type of arrangement was the tuzzy-muzzy, a small circular bouquet carried by Victorian ladies, in which several kinds of small blooms were placed in perfect concentric circles according to colour and variety. The concoction was edged with some sort of foliage, a lace frill, or perhaps even paper lace, and finally placed in a special bouquet holder, made of porcelain, enamel-ware or precious metal. An added attraction of this type of bouquet was that it could be employed as a means of communication, in the flower language mentioned above. This lamentable style of arrangement has survived until the present day in the shape of the traditional bridesmaid's bouquet.

Many of the women's publications arbitrated on the choice of suitable flowers for all occasions and appropriate containers, and gave helpful suggestions for arrangement and maintenance. Indeed, a nice judgment in suiting the flowers to the vase and to each other was considered essential in anyone who aspired to good taste, and those who did deplored overcrowding and the moribund, claustrophic atmosphere of the houses of the rich who were not obliged to fall back on natural materials for ornament. Subsequently it became fashionable to use wild grasses and leaves in certain compositions, and it was considered essential to include some form of foliage in all arrangements. An appreciation of Nature also became a necessary part of any child's education. The children of middle-class and aristocratic families had lessons in botany and horticulture and the girls had to attempt watercolours of well-known garden plants. They also kept scrap-book collections of flower prints and pressed flowers. The level of the average housewife's knowledge of flowers was therefore higher than it is today, and it was even considered a mark of ill-breeding to be ignorant in the field. Interest in cultivating and cross-breeding plants reached a high level among amateurs, while conservatories were added on to houses at a great rate, so that people could experiment with exotic plants that could not survive the northern climate.

As may be imagined, the Victorians turned their technical skills to making a wide range of flower containers, though they also imported many from the Orient. Glass was much used – cut, blown, etched, moulded and pressed in a variety of shapes and patterns. There was gilded glass, coloured glass, milk glass, painted and enamelled glass. Other vases were made of hand-painted porcelain with applied modelling, and cheaper versions in glazed or unglazed moulded pottery. Traditional ornamental vases were made of marble, alabaster and metal, many of them based on Italian Renaissance designs. Urns and tall épergnes with trumpet flared tops were fashioned in cast iron and painted white or brilliant colours. Some of the larger containers, such as jardinières, were fitted with metal liners in which foliage plants and moss were grown, providing a permanent background for cut flowers. Special stands made of wood, bamboo and wickerwork, again fitted with metal or pottery liners, were used for keeping pot plants in dining and drawing rooms. Some households possessed special flower containers in china to match their dinner service – according to Mrs Beeton, this was the last word in chic.

Numerous rules governing the art of flower decoration were put forward by would-be authorities on taste, etiquette and *savoir faire*. Julia Berrall quotes from the *St. Nicholas Magazine* (a periodical publication for girls) some advice on how to achieve striking contrasts with colour: a large vase was first of all to be divided into thirds, then you should 'arrange a group of maroon, scarlet, and white geraniums [a colour to a section, presumably] with green leaves, and add a single blossom of gold coloured calceolaria, and you will see at once that the whole bouquet seems to flash out and become more brilliant'. Mrs Beeton naturally had views on appropriate arrangements for the dining table. 'Where the means of the housekeeper or the supply of flowers is limited, delicate-looking ferns, Japanese dwarf trees, and other plants suitable for table use may be employed, for they look in many cases as pretty as flowers, unless the latter be most tastefully arranged. Maiden-hair looks perhaps prettier than ordinary ferns, but will not stand the heat of a dining-room so well'. She warns against the use of heavily scented flowers with her usual tact: 'To some the perfume of such flowers as gardenias, stephanotis, hyacinths and others is not offensive, but to others the strong scent in a heated room, especially during dinner, is considered very unpleasant'. Mrs Beeton also disapproved of too many different colours in one arrangement, preferring two only, and underlining the effectiveness of white flowers mixed with greenery. She comments on the current vogue for having a single colour for the table decoration, adding that it was 'often chosen of the same tint as the hostess's dress or the hangings of the room, though these are sometimes varied to suit the flowers'.

There were so many schools of taste in the last decades of the 19th century that it is difficult to generalise. The most obvious distinction can be seen in the contrasting tastes of the bohemian intellectuals and the solid middle- or upper-class family: the former's allegiance wavered between the effete, elongated, lily shapes and pallid colours of the *Art Nouveau* school, the haunted, mediaeval gloom of the Pre-Raphaelites, and the folk-art 'simplicity' of William Morris. Their ideal surroundings were unlikely to include overburdened plant stands or a surfeit of crammed vases – instead there would perhaps have been a slender vessel of iridescent glass, containing a single, perfect bloom, placed on a spindly side-table. The atmosphere in ordinary family surroundings would have been altogether less restrained. A description by Osbert Lancaster in *Here of All Places* of the use of plants in interior decoration in what he calls 'The Earnest 'Eighties' perfectly expresses what one could have expected. 'But perhaps the most striking feature of the period is the extraordinary love of plant-life which manifests itself in every interior. Aspidistras, palms, rubber-plants and every variety of fern thrive and flourish on all sides, while, no longer living but still decorative, the bullrush disputes with the pampas grass the possession of the costliest available vase. Dimly through the jungle half-light one perceives on the walls, in very wide gold mounts, the exquisite water-colours of Mr Birket Foster and many talented studies of irises and other artistic flowers by the young lady of the house. And when the gas is turned up and all the myriad green leaves, swaying in time to the strains of Balfe or of Tosti cast strange shadows on the chrysanthemum-covered wall, one would fancy oneself in some tropical fairyland as yet unpenetrated by the dauntless Doctor Livingstone.'

The 1914–18 War finally administered the long overdue death blow to Victorianism and its more unfortunate restrictions and tasteless excesses in the artistic field, too many of which continued to flourish in the freer atmosphere of the Edwardian era. Straitened circumstances after the war forced many people to abandon their formal – and expensive – way of life for a more bohemian style. There was a renewed interest in Oriental styles, because remarkable effects could be achieved with great economy of time, money and materials. Chinese, Japanese, and Slav furnishings and *objets* became popular, and studio-type houses, which were comparatively easy to maintain without domestic servants, were considered ideal residences.

The lady of the house now found herself obliged to spend a great deal of time and effort on household chores, with correspondingly less time to devote to domestic arts. There was, too, the effect of the emancipation of women, which engendered a degree of scorn for lady-like accomplishments and encouraged women to compete with men in more intellectual fields. Inevitably, interest in flower arrangement waned and there were few developments. The tendency was to adhere to old styles, or simply to place a few flowers at random in a jug, in the *style nature* so often depicted by Sir William Nicholson (1872–1949), an English painter of portraits, landscapes, and particularly still-lifes. However, women did wear flowers during this period, and it was customary for men to offer a *corsage* when he escorted a woman for an evening. Expensive flowers such as camellias, gardenias and orchids showed sophisticated taste, but roses and carnations were more frequently used. The corsage was made up of a few blooms wired together with leaves or *asparagus plumosa* and was pinned to the bodice of the dress. The more flamboyant versions were embellished with elaborate bows of satin or velvet ribbon. This fashion reached its peak in the 'thirties and 'forties, and declined in the 'fifties, though the corsage is still sometimes worn nowadays for special occasions, particularly weddings.

The Paris Exhibition of Decorative Arts in 1925 established a style based on pure curves and simple decoration, characterised by an abundant use of textiles with geometrical designs taken from the Cubists, and Art Nouveau floral patterns. On the whole it was a dreary period for interiors: the trend towards plainness meant that much of the clutter of objects that had filled interiors during the preceding decades was eliminated, but the changes were hardly drastic. The time had come when designers felt that something original should be 'said', but they had not yet decided what this should be. Only when the work of Le Corbusier, Mies Van der Rohe, Gropius on the Continent and Frank Lloyd Wright in America came to the fore did a new aesthetic exist in a positive sense. Needless to say, the language of a new style had been developing since the war, but it had made little impact as its adherents and exponents were confined to the culturally élite avant-garde. (True, the work of Le Corbusier became known in his design for the Pavilion de L'Esprit Nouveau at the 1925 Exhibition, but this was at the time an exception to prevailing trends.)

The architectural revolution produced a functional style distinguished by severe linear forms and an absence of ornamentation. Interiors became bare, clean, brightly lit and rather box-like; furniture and furnishings were sparse. The fashionable approach to flower arrangement during this period was directly influenced by these austere surroundings. Containers were devoid of ornament and designed in simple, geometrical shapes, chiefly the cylinder, cube and sphere, sometimes with slight modifications; they were often made of thick glass or hand-thrown stoneware pottery. Unnatural colouring and decoration was frowned upon by the purists, so clear glass and unglazed pottery were preferred, although pale primary colours and rough glazing were just acceptable. Primitive pottery became fashionable, and modern designs were produced by old methods.

Japanese design has played an important role in the shaping of 20th century Western taste in many fields, industrial as well as artistic, but perhaps one of the most lasting effects has been that of *Ikebana* the Japanese art of flower arranging. Like Chinese flower arranging, *Ikebana* is a very ancient traditional art with a religious and philosophical background. The first arrangements were created in the 6th century by a Buddhist priest, Ono-no-Imoko. He felt that it was not sufficient to place flowers carelessly before Buddha, and determined to make symbolic arrangements. For many hundreds of years after this, flowers were only arranged for the temples by priests and a style evolved (called *Rikka*) in which the arrangements could tower up to as much as twenty feet, taking weeks to complete. Subsequently flower arrangements appeared at the Imperial Court, and aroused so much interest that the nobles took up flower arranging at home. In present-day Japan every woman, regardless of social standing, must study *Ikebana*, but until the middle of the 19th century it was an exclusively male pursuit, and even now, although many women teach the art, men are still the Grand Masters of most schools.

Classical Japanese flower arrangement is divided into two schools: *Rikka* (or *Rikkwa*) the ancient temple art, and *Ikenobo*, which falls into various sub-divisions according to the degree of formality. *Rikka* arrangements have been reduced to a more manageable size than the original versions, but are nonetheless extremely complicated and apparently take *at least* three or four hours to complete. Their distinguishing characteristic is that the plant material stands up very stiffly in its container. *Ikenobo* arrangements – the name is that of the oldest school of flower arrangement in Japan – are based on the expression of three elements: (1) principal or Heaven, (2) streamer or man, (3) recipient or Earth, each of which is represented by different pieces, placed in strict relationship to each other and to the container as regards height and angle. As far as the guiding principles of *Ikebana* are concerned, it is believed that artistic satisfaction can only be achieved with integrity, and the commonest weed, thoughtfully and gracefully arranged, can be as successful as the most magnificent flower. (In fact weeds have an advantage, in that the risk of ostentation is minimal.) All arrangements must be made from seasonal materials (in order that they should harmonize with the view through the outer glass doors of a Japanese house) and are therefore representational – in following Nature – as well as decorative. Formal arrangements should always create an illusion of spontaneous growth. In order to achieve this effect, correct relative heights should be observed: a flower must never tower over a tree branch, a mountain plant should be placed above a field plant, a field plant above a water plant, and so on. The level of water in the vase varies according to the season, and the choice of vase itself is governed by convention.

The first recorded treatise on Japanese flower arrangement was written by a 12th century Master of *Ikenobo*. This work has been revised and added to over the centuries, but many of the basic rules and conventions set out in it remain the same. Some of the rules are as follows: it is forbidden to take too many flowers from the garden; forbidden to wear a white costume while arranging them; and forbidden to criticize unceremoniously an arrangement created by another person. (Perhaps 'forbidden' is too strong a word in this context: 'considered ill-mannered, uncivilised and dishonourable' would probably be more accurate.) The regulations also specify that one should maintain a dignified and graceful posture while arranging flowers, and that no one should ever praise his own arrangement. Warning is given against arranging flowers while in a state of anxiety, hostility or spiritual depression, because an arrangement is a mirror of the soul and it would be supremely anti-social behaviour to inflict one's personal disquiet on others.

No one has influenced contemporary English flower arranging as much as Constance Spry. Mrs Spry began her career as a free-lance flower decorator, opened a florist shop in London during the 'thirties, and wrote many books on gardening and flower arrangement. She was an artist of skill, talent and taste, and an articulate, disciplined and energetic teacher. Her books remain among the best in the field, in spite of changing fashions and the availability of new equipment. Mrs Spry initiated a style of arrangement characterised by a generous use of material and a new freedom in displaying it. A typical Constance Spry mass arrangement or bouquet is baroque by comparison with the tightly ordered and symmetrically arranged decorations of the Victorian period and the ascetic vases of the 'twenties. Indeed, some of the larger arrangements are reminiscent of Dutch flower-piece paintings of the early 17th century, particularly the spontaneous, un-mannered bouquets painted by Bruegel, De Heem, and the German-born Mignon. These mass arrangements are rich in colour and texture; there is great variety of depth, and the outline, usually based on a circle or semi-circle, is open and exuberantly disarrayed.

Constance Spry's work represents a break from convention and illustrates an originality of expression which is so characteristic of the 20th century. It also emphasises the transfer from men to women of much of the responsibility for making aesthetic decisions in interior decoration. In the introductory chapter of *Flowers in House and Garden* (first published 1937, J. M. Dent & Sons, Ltd.) Mrs Spry remarks that, until the end of the 19th century, 'one's house was almost a life sentence. Once committed to expensive papers, the best shiny paint, to hung velvet or brocade, it was not much use to get tired of the result, and since the initial choice would often lie between the master of the house and the "painter and decorator", it was sometimes possible for the mistress of the house to be bored even before she started to live with it.' She goes on to point out that cut flowers were valued more for sentimental reasons than for their decorative potential: 'It is only recently that flowers have come to be treated as decorative materials, to be used as an artist uses paint, or even as a sculptor clay.'

The value of continual, unprejudiced experiment, with colours and combinations of materials, the consideration of a flower-piece as an artefact created for a particular setting or even as the focal point of the room – not merely a space-filler, but an integral part of the decor – and a disregard for rules and conventions: these are principles which Mrs Spry feels should govern any attempt to create flower decorations. She also emphasises the importance of manual dexterity and practical experience in handling the materials and equipment, stressing the point that no amateur should delude herself (or himself) with the idea that it is possible to achieve an effect with the efficiency of a professional florist, whose craft is learned through the course of a long apprenticeship. Her treatment of the whole subject is factual and technical, on the assumption that it is reasonable to teach people about the nature of materials and how to handle them, but impossible to impart the essence of creative imagination to wooden-hearted philistines: taste can be educated and talent awakened only when there is visual sensitivity.

Constance Spry's 'school' of flower arrangement, as it existed in her day, formed the basis from which the art as it is practised in England today has developed. The work of the most creative and original of contemporary English flower arrangers has carried further the trend towards informality. There is, too, a current enthusiasm for reproducing period arrangements, done, not in the spirit of imitation, but of interpretation.

Increased efficiency in transport in recent years has made possible greater originality and experimentation in the field of flower decoration, as now even the most exotic plants can be easily acquired, if at some expense. Cultivation techniques are undergoing intensive research and study, with the result that flowers can be grown more cheaply now than ever before (regardless of season); hardier varieties of existing strains are being produced and many new and exciting variants appear every year. These factors all contribute to the astonishing renaissance of the art of flower arranging today.

technical aspects

Ideally, flower arranging equipment should be kept in one place, preferably in a small room, complete with sink and a large working surface. It is useful to have two buckets, one shallow for small stems, the other deep for unwieldy branches. The latter should be heavy so that it will not tip over easily. Market flowers bought off barrows or from florists should be immediately immersed in water, so at least one bucket, detergent-free and exclusively for flowers, is vital, unless you always pick them fresh from the garden. It is essential that all market flowers, particularly roses, should be steeped in deep water in a cool, dark place, *at least* overnight.

It is preferable to do the actual arrangement *in situ*, unless you have a particularly accurate visual memory, because the colours of the setting will continue to influence what you are doing while you are in the process of doing it.

The most effective way to keep flowers in position is to support them with 2-inch mesh wire netting, fitted into the vase. Most ironmongers stock this in rolls and stubby-bladed florist's scissors, or ordinary shears, make light work of the cutting. (Netting is generally far superior to other holders like kenzans, which tend to tip over). To fit the wire, cut a piece more than twice the size of the vase's base and crumple it into several layers so that the holes overlap. If the holes are too large, the flowers tend to slip, but they can be made secure if each stem is held by wire at several levels. To hold the netting in place, hook it over the edge of the vase or fasten it with a fine wire looped through and tied around or under the vase. A dust-sheet is indispensable: first, for transporting the flowers, secondly, to protect the floor or surface where you are working, and thirdly, for removing the debris. Proper cutting tools are very important, too. There is nothing more frustrating than trying to cut woody stems with feeble kitchen scissors. The best all-purpose scissors are florists' scissors, which are well-balanced with short, tough, sharp blades. All stems should be trimmed before they are steeped in water prior to arrangement, because they will have sealed up. Woody stems slit a couple of inches up the middle from the base will last noticeably longer. Provided that all fresh flower arrangements are topped

up daily, a complete change of water is unnecessary, but remember that woody stemmed species need as much as two refills a day.

Before beginning an arrangement, decide from which angles it will be seen most. If it is to be against a wall, for instance, begin by positioning the background foliage and work forwards. Do not forget that it must also be well-composed from the side view. Free-standing arrangements, like a table centre-piece, are seen from all sides, from above and almost at eye-level. Flowers are like actors on a round stage and should never turn their backs to the audience. The first step when working out a composition, is to create a rough outline by inserting the largest and longest pieces first. Lighting plays an important part in any arrangement and can alter colour and texture quite dramatically. It is therefore advisable, if sometimes inconvenient, to work in the same light as that in which the finished arrangement will be seen for most of the time. Never cross the stems of flowers. Each piece should be free-standing, otherwise there is a risk that if one piece moves, it will disarrange the whole vase. Free-standing flowers also look more natural. Crushed together, the subtle interplay of forms is obscured and the vase will look crammed, probably messy, and certainly boring. Do not hack off stems indiscriminately in an attempt to force your material into a preconceived design, or because it is awkward to handle. Thoughtless pruning can eliminate interesting possibilities.

As with any art form, the eye has to be trained to really *see*, and there is nothing like practice for training it. First, dispense with self-consciousness and do not expect to make an immortal contribution to art with the first try. Ideas are self-generating and a single attempt to arrange a bunch of flowers thoughtfully, instead of pushing them willy-nilly into a handy container, can be enough to awaken interest. Skill comes only by repetition and by learning from the work of others. Arranging flowers can be an absorbing and creative pastime and is one of the few arts that can give great satisfaction to a mediocre talent.

The choice of container is a personal one and the following notes are merely personal views on the subject, which we hope will prove helpful and not discourage further experiment. Some examples are illustrated. For instance, an urn-shaped vase and pedestal are suitable for mass arrangements such as those often used to decorate a church for a wedding. For a dining table centre-piece, it is advisable to use a low bowl; a round bowl looks well on a circular, oval or square table, while an oblong container is better for a long table. China and porcelain vases look light and fragile and suit small, delicate arrangements. But if you are convinced heavier material would look right, the base of the vase can be weighted with sand. Baskets with metal or glass liners make attractive containers for arrangements of wild flowers or spring flowers, fixed in loose, disarrayed compositions. Cornflowers, daisies, marigolds and primroses have an inherent simplicity which is brought out by an unpretentious, unglazed pot. Epergnes, loaded with fruit, are extremely effective for decorating a sideboard or buffet table, although the result may have a slightly self-conscious 'period' ring.

Objects not intended to hold flowers can look pretty, unusual or fun: tea caddies, wine coolers, glass goblets, metal or ceramic jugs, drinking mugs, silver fruit baskets, to name only a few. In fact, almost any container can be used as a vase, provided that you can overcome the practical problems of making it waterproof. A simple glass bowl can always be used as a liner, but avoid using priceless alabaster, glass and silver, since they are easily stained by plant decomposition. A daily change of water for valuable containers helps to diminish the corrosion but it can never be completely eliminated. While original containers can be used with great flair, beware of clichés or of creating a ridiculous or *recherché* result. For instance, copper pots have been vastly over-used and have rural connotations which would be inappropriate to a London flat or skyscraper apartment. Consider the setting and decide what is appropriate to the atmosphere. It is a cardinal rule that a flower arrangement must be designed as an integral part of its setting, acting as a catalyst for surrounding colours, textures and forms; it must never, like flambé dishes prepared noisily at the table, dominate the conversation and outshine the room's contents – people included.

Arranging flowers, has become a far easier and more enjoyable task in recent times. Original vases from Spain and Italy have revitalised many a gift department in the large stores. English pottery, well represented at the London Craft Centre, tends to be less colourful but it is rich and exuberant in its own way. Equipment, too, has improved and become more readily available. There is currently some useful research being done on methods of keeping cut flowers fresh for longer periods, so it is worth trying out new products as they come on the market.

drying, pressing and preserving

The easiest material to dry by hanging.

The true everlastings: Acrolinium, Helichrysum (both need to be wired first), Rhodanthe, Zeranthemum, Statice (*bonduelli* and *sinuatia*), Statice (*guielini* and *latifolium*), Ammobium, Artichoke.

Other varieties: Annaphalis, Achillea, Stachys lanata, Hydrangea (dry standing upright in very little water), Lunaria.

Good seedheads (cultivated): Poppy, Iris, Tulip, Nigella, Foxglove, Onion, Leek, Radish, Grape Hyacinth, Bluebell, Corn cobs.

Good seedheads (wild): Knapweed, Wall Cress, Thistles, Plantains, Hog Weed, Teazle (scan the fields, woods and hedgerows for these as well as other seedheads to try).

Grasses both wild and cultivated should be dried standing upright in an empty container. Gathered early in the season and dried in a dark place, much of their true colour is preserved.

Foliage suitable for drying in Glycerine: Beech, Oak, Sweet Chestnut, Laurel, Hawthorn, Mahonia, 'Old Man's Beard', Eucalyptus, Privet. (All these should be cut in late summer, but before the insects start to eat them. When dried they take on various shades of brown).

The drying and preserving of flowers demands a degree of patience and skill which does little to recommend it to the impatient amateur or, for that matter, the busy professional. The processes involved are laborious and, once treated, the material is extremely fragile, ready to disintegrate in all but the steadiest fingers. Working with dried material is really an art in itself and, while an expert can achieve the same effects as an arranger working with fresh materials, the enthusiastic amateur must realise that the techniques are as dissimilar as those employed in, say, *petit-point* and knitting.

There are three basic methods of 'drying' flowers and foliage: drying, preserving and pressing. The first of these is the simplest and needs less time, skill and experience to produce satisfactory results; however, it has the disadvantage of being suited to a limited range of material. The material, gathered into loose bunches, is tied at the base of the stems and then strung on a clothes line in a dry, well-ventilated room or cupboard, *away from heat.* Adequate ventilation is essential or mould will appear. Drying time depends largely on air circulation and the weather; naturally, the more fleshy the plant the longer it will take to dry. Material dried by hanging will become straight, so where natural curves are required, as with grasses, the material should be stood in a container and allowed to dry in the same conditions.

Drying in glycerine is recommended for foliages like beech, oak, hawthorn, chestnut and laurel. The branches are prepared by crushing the base of the stems and leaving them in a deep bucket of luke-warm water overnight. This ensures that they will draw fluid. Mix glycerine in solution in the ratio of one pint of glycerine to two pints of hot water and pour into a bucket. The branches should be immersed up to six or seven inches, measured from the bottom of the stems, taking care not to overcrowd, because this will produce mould. Leave them for at least a week, until the leaves have turned a brownish colour. Beautiful, rich colours can be encouraged by exposing the branches to light while they are soaking up the glycerine and by spreading them in the sun after they have been removed. The main advantage of this method is that, in contrast to the hanging method, the material will not become brittle.

Leaves and ferns are best treated by pressing. Each piece should be laid flat between large sheets of absorbent paper. Make sure that they do not touch each other or overlap and that they are in the position you want them to be when dried. Placed under heavy weights – large books are best – they should be left in a dry place for several weeks. The advantage of pressing is that the material tends to preserve its colours. After pressing, the leaves can be wired (ivy leaves often are) by interweaving a fine florist's wire at points in the back of the leaf's central spine. Fine wire wrapped several times around the central spine of ferns and bracken, once pressed, renders them firm and pliable. Ferns for pressing should be gathered when mature as young ferns are too thin and fragile. Many can be sprayed and painted, and look particularly pretty silvered or gilded in Christmas decorations.

Material suitable for pressing: Bracken (green and golden), 'Ladder Fern', Ivy, Raspberry, Senecio, Echinops, Royal Fern.

There are two ways of preserving flowers, apart from straight-forward drying, glycerine drying and pressing. One is by borax and the other by silica gel. Borax is cheaper to buy in quantity, but used over a long period may cause eye and skin allergies. Silica gel is more expensive but easier to use. In both cases, loop a florist's wire unobtrusively through the head of each flower, making a short, fake stalk which can be added to subsequently in the flower arranging process. The wire makes the preserved flowers easier to manipulate, and without this added strengthener they are almost too brittle to position accurately. Put a deep bed of borax powder on the bottom of a cardboard box – deep enough to hold the wire stems in position. Having 'planted' the flower heads, making sure they do not touch each other, spoon the powder over and inside each head and between each petal. Take great care not to bend, bruise or alter the petals' natural angles. Store the cardboard box in a hot, dry place, without a lid, for at least forty-eight hours and up to three days. Use a fine sable brush to remove the powder from the petals. Pink flowers tend to turn mauve in borax and it is not a good method to use for roses.

Flowers to preserve in Borax or Silica Gel: These methods make flowers brittle, so choose those with fairly thick petals. Among the best are Gentian, Delphinium (especially 'Blue Bees'), Hellebore, Zinnia. Borax is not as good for roses as Silica Gel. Results vary with different types of roses, but good ones to try are Tawny Gold, Sweet Seventeen, Super Star, Chiffon, Carol (this variety tends to turn mauve).

Flowers are packed into silica gel in exactly the same way, except that the containers must be *airtight*. Once packed, seal the lids of the containers with sellotape, store them at normal room temperature and leave from three to six days, depending on the fleshiness of the material: for example, delphiniums will need longer than roses. After being used three or four times, silica gel will start to turn blue. When this happens, spread it out on a tin to dry in a cool oven for about two-and-a-half hours. It should then be cooled and stored in an airtight tin. Store your dried material in plastic bags in a damp-proof room with ample space around it. Its fragility cannot be overstressed.

The arrangement of dried material, particularly flowers, is an extremely delicate business. Begin by making a holder in the base of the vase: a powder detergent mixed to the consistency of wall-plugging putty is ideal, because of its slow setting action; but if you are arranging any quantity of small, dried flowers, it is more economical to give the vase a false cardboard bottom by cutting a circle of thickish cardboard and sticking it with glue about two inches below the lip of the vase. The positioning of the false bottom

Mass arrangement of all dried and preserved material at the foot of the staircase in a Tudor cottage in London. The container, an iron urn, has been placed on a marble column. Material used in this arrangement includes Hydrangeas, Zinnias, Peonies, Achillea, Love-lies-bleeding (Amaranthus caudatus), Agapanthus, Honesty (Lunaria), Chinese Lanterns (Physalis), Acanthus, Globe artichoke flowers (Cynara scolymus), Corn-cobs, Teazles, Magnolia leaves, Lichen-covered branches, Pampas grass (Cortaderia), various wild grasses.

can only be judged by common sense, taking into account the weight of the material and the appearance of the vase.

Glass vases can be filled with moss, on which is placed the cardboard covered with a bed of prepared paste. This is camouflaged with dried moss, in which the flowers are then arranged. If unwired dried material, such as statice, is to stand up very straight in an arrangement, wire should be wrapped around the stems as for fresh flowers. Avoid wiring, whenever possible, because it exaggerates the stiff, brittle quality of dried material. The natural postures of flowers add grace to these potentially gloomy, mummified compositions.

As always, choose containers to suit the contents. Autumn leaves, pressed bracken and seed heads look well in stone or copper pots; preserved roses and gentians suit pretty, fragile china baskets or vases. If the arrangement may have to be moved, make sure that the vase has a base or stem and can be carried easily. Never try to arrange small dried flowers in a hurry. Even someone with great experience in working with this sort of material will take approximately two-and-a-half hours to complete a composition.

The field of drying and preserving is in desperate need of research, so do not be afraid to deviate from the suggested list to improve on old methods or to explore new ones. Ways to reduce the fragility of dried plants are badly needed and we still have not discovered how to preserve flowers with very thin petals.

spring

Spring is a slow awakening. The hardy bulbs appear first: crocuses, snowdrops, daffodils, jonquils, narcissi and hyacinths. Crocuses look deceptively fragile, as though once cut they would die; but in fact they last quite well and, arranged with small ferns, moss, forsythia and pieces of bark or driftwood, look no less enchanting indoors than they do under the trees. Snowdrops sometimes flower in late December; the variety known as *Galanthus caucasicus* is the earliest. Their bell-shaped heads with tiny green markings on each petal make them delicate material for miniature arrangements on a dressing-table or desk, or in flat dishes lined with moss. Hyacinths are easily forced indoors in pots, but tend to look better cut and arranged in a vase, as their heads droop. Daffodils (which belong to the genus *Narcissus*) like many other spring flowers look best on their own, arranged simply with greenery. Tulips, another hardy spring bulb, lend themselves to more grandiose mass arrangements. Violets, which are very fragile and wilt quickly out of water, but

A funeral wreath. Bunches of Primula and Snowdrops arranged loosely on a circular base of wire mesh and moss, with Ivy trails. The photograph was taken in a Wiltshire churchyard.

smell delicious, will last longer if you dip their heads in cold water for a few minutes before arranging.

Several species of *Helleborus* flower in the early spring. Sometimes, ironically, if the winter is particularly severe, the Christmas Rose (*H. niger*) does not flower until late winter, although, forced or imported, it is usually available in the markets and shops by Christmas, if you are willing to pay the price. But it is the green varieties which are most valuable to the flower arranger: stinking hellebore (*H. foetidus*), green hellebore (*H. viridis*) and *H. corsicus* all flower in the very early spring. These varieties mix well in large pedestal arrangements with small groups of early spring flowers, and even with dried material. The Lenten Rose (*H. orientalis*), although not long lasting, has attractive, open-faced flowers in different shades of mauve and white, often with subtle brown spotted marking. All hellebores should be arranged in deep water, or they last no time at all.

A small, informal arrangement in a country bedroom composed of cream, blue and white Hyacinths combined with berried Ivy and Artichoke leaves.

A funeral wreath of mixed Hyacinths with Ivy.

Blossom branches are a gift to any flower arranger, but they must be cut with great care and discretion to avoid damaging the tree. The branches grow in beautiful shapes which immediately give form and dynamism to an arrangement. The colour and texture of the blossoms are delicate, subtle and sensuous. Apple and cherry blossom (especially *Prunus serrulata*) looks handsome in simple arrangements mixed with a few branches of foliage, in mixed groups, or even alone in a rather severe arrangement, if you have a talent for linear composition. The evergreen foliage of rhododendrons is useful all the year round. The genus *Rhododendron* covers a large family of shrubs, including the azaleas. As a result of much hybridizing, the blossoms can now be found in practically any colour, even yellow.

Among the first spring foliages are early beech, and several species of weeping willow (*Salix vitellina pendula*), which have attractive plumed branches that add character to large groups.

A table arrangement for the entrance hall of a country house. Daffodils and yellow and white Narcissi, combined with Guelder rose (Viburnum opulus), variegated Ivy, Artichoke leaves and branches of crab-apple blossom.

A large group of spring flowers in a Roman vase, photographed in the entrance hall of a house in Wiltshire (c.1670). Daffodils and Forsythia set against a background of Pussy Willow (Salix discolor) with Ivy trails.

28

The pussy willow (*S. discolor*) which, strictly speaking, is neither foliage nor flower, can be found in the hedgerows in early spring and is particularly effective with daffodils, tulips and irises. Larch (*Larix decidua*) is beginning to shoot in this season and has fresh bright green needles and small terracotta coloured cones along its gracefully curved branches. This, too, is good background material for large mixed compositions.

In a sense, spring is the most exciting season for flower arrangement: the flowers and leaves have a quality of freshness that is obscured later by the rococo flamboyance of summer, and the availability of wild material means that much less reliance need be placed on the vagaries of the market. The resulting arrangements are inevitably less contrived, less complicated and pedantic than those created during the winter months – and perhaps more inspired.

In principle, decorations for early spring weddings must rely on imported material: white lilac, guelder rose (*Viburnum opulus*), camellias, lilies, freesias (which first appear in the shops before Christmas), hyacinths and varieties of evergreen *Prunus*. For bouquets, attractive effects can be achieved with camellias, freesias, forced lily-of-the-valley, hyacinths and rhododendron blooms, removed from the stem and wired. By late spring, the majority of blossoms, flowers and foliage for church decoration can be gathered from the garden and countryside.

Drawing-room table arrangement of Green Hellebore (Helleborus viridis), in a Spanish terracotta pot.

Church decoration for an early spring wedding. Most of the material for this arrangement was imported because of the shortage of seasonal long-stemmed flowers and blossom. White Lilac (from France) with a white Azalea plant, Lilies (Lilium longiflorum harrisii), Guelder roses, Variegated Laurel (Prunus lusitanica variegata), Cherry Laurel (P. laurocerasus), Rhododendron, Ivy, and Hazel catkins.

A small arrangement of Parrot Tulips, combined with Megasea leaves (Bergenia crassifolia), St. John's Wort berries (Hypericum calycinum), and berried Ivy. This piece was photographed in the entrance hall of a house in Wiltshire. The arrangement seen through the doorway in the Grinling Gibbons (1648–1721) room appears on p.34.

A table centrepiece in an Adam dining-room. Here a garland made of Camellias in red and varying shades of pink, with Ivy trails and White Flowering Jasmine (Jasminum officinale) was used to decorate this long table with twelve place settings. The shades harmonize with the green and muted rose colour scheme of the furnishings. The loose sprawling composition of the garland gives a light touch to the formal elegance of the room. A garland is an excellent type of decoration for a long table as it is quicker to arrange than several separate vases and can be prepared well ahead of time and kept in water to be put into place at the last minute.

An extravagant formal drawing-room group for an oak panelled room in a house in Wiltshire with carvings by Grinling Gibbons. The container is a large brass urn. Included in the arrangement are Amaryllis, 'Super Star' roses, Darwin Tulips, Euphorbia fulgens, pale pink Rhododendron, a Pelargonium plant ('Apple Dawn'), Senecio, branches of Dogwood (Cornus), Eucalyptus leaves (E. populifolius), and Hazel catkins. This photograph was taken in front of a door in order to show the magnificent carving; the arrangement can be seen in its correct position in the illustration on p.32.

Dining-table centrepiece. A planted dish, using simple fresh spring material: Primula (P. auricula), Hellebore, Witch-Hazel (Hamamelis mollis), and Ladder fern (Nephrolepsis exaltata), with Lichen moss. In the background is a still-life by Willem van Aelst. The room was decorated by Hopton & Patching.

Opposite page

A decorated marquee for a spring wedding in the country. In the foreground is one of the four central pillars; these were covered with pink and red Camellias. The large group on a torchère in the corner is composed of Crown Imperials (Fritillaria imperialis), *Kaffir lilies* (Clivia), *Amaryllis, Guelder Rose* (Viburnum opulus), *yellow single Chrysanthemums, pink Crab-apple blossom, pink Rhododendron, and Berberis, with trails of variegated Ivy.*

A church decoration for a spring wedding in the country. This is one of two large mass arrangements which were placed on the chancel steps in pedestal vases. The material used is very colourful and includes Crown Imperials (Fritillaria imperialis), Kaffir Lilies (Clivia), yellow single Chrysanthemums, pink Snapdragons (Anti-rrhinum), and Tiger Lilies.

Opposite page

A hall decoration for a wedding reception in a Georgian country house. The simple massed bouquet arranged in a polished wood urn combines varying shades of pink Rhododendron with branches of pink Crab-apple blossom.

Previous page

*A low informal arrangement of Rhodo-
dendron and Azalea blooms in various
shades of red and pink. The container is an
antique copper cooking kettle. Its warm
glow blends well with the colour of the
flowers and the rosewood table top.*

*A Bridesmaid's bouquet made from pale
pink Rhododendron flowers removed from
the stem and wired.*

*A loose, fan-shaped arrangement for a spring wedding, combining Regalia (*Lilium regale*) and* Longiflorum *Lilies, Rhododendron, Magnolia,* Echeveria *and sprays of wild and Japanese cherry blossom.*

43

Below

An informal arrangement of white Bluebells in a white painted wicker basket (with a metal liner).

Opposite page

A decoration for a wedding reception at Claridge's Hotel in London. This arrangement was one of a pair which stood on either side of the cake table. The pyramid-shaped mass bouquet, arranged in a black cast iron urn mounted on a black marble column pedestal, is composed of dark pink 'lily flowering' Tulips, parrot Tulips, pink and mauve Rhododendrons (with their foliage), pink Azaleas (also with their foliage), coral and pale pink Carnations, Guelder rose (Viburnum opulus), with trails of ivy. At the apex of the arrangement is a bunch of Ladder Fern.

Left

An arrangement for the entrance hall to an apartment in London which is decorated in Japanese style: the walls are covered with a reddish-gold printed fabric. The dark woodwork is lacquered, and the floor is tiled in marble. The container for this enormous composition of apple blossom, *moss and logs is an antique Japanese bell, nearly four feet high. The blossom branches are so beautifully shaped that they almost arrange themselves, and a handsome effect can be achieved with very few pieces.*

Above

A drawing-room group in a modern apartment in London. The flowers were *arranged in a huge Spanish black pottery container and placed on a glass-topped coffee table. The bouquet is loose and casual in composition. The material includes Enchantment Lilies (Lilium umbellatum), 'Golden Clarion' Lilies, Crown Imperials (Fritillaria imperialis), Green Hellebore, Berberis, Himalayan Rhododendron leaves and branches of Sycamore.*

Previous page

Below

Right

A table arrangement for a modern London flat. Longiflorum *lilies are combined with* Solomon's Seal *(Polygonatum multi-florum) and green* Hellebore (Helleborus viridis).

A free and natural looking bowl of Marguerites for a modern apartment.

A brightly coloured Anemone 'tree'. This type of bouquet is uncluttered and particularly successful where the arrangement will be free-standing or, as here, reflected in mirrors.

Table centrepieces for the modern dining-room in Mrs Leonard Lewis's house in London. Bunches of bright orange Marigolds (Calendula) were chosen to pick up the colour in the painting on the left-hand wall which dominates the pale monochrome room with its steel and glass dining table. The flowers were tightly arranged in miniature compotes of white Italian pottery, keeping a simple line, in harmony with the stark, spacious character of the room.

A decorated cake table for a wedding reception in London. The table was covered with a bouffante organdie cloth and garlanded with small bouquets of wired white Hyacinth florets with Ivy trails. On the top of the cake is a tiny bunch of white Hyacinth florets, Lily-of-the-Valley (Convallaria majalis) and moss. In the background is one of the two large pedestal groups which flanked the table.

summer

A table group in a low oak butter bowl, in muted shades of green, silver and pale pink. Combined here are Heath (Erica), *Senecio,* Artichoke *leaves,* Garrya elliptica *catkins and variegated Box.*

A simple desk bouquet of double Ranunculus *in a black Spanish pot.*

The variety of flowers available at this time of year justifies the expansiveness of summer arrangements. Generous groups of lush flowers in a riot of different colours are in tune with the warmth and gaiety of the season, and, when the sun does not appear, bowls laden with flowers can help to compensate for a day spent indoors. Simple seasonal arrangements of wild flowers and grasses look cool and soothing on the hottest day. Arrangements of mixed greenery

gathered from fields, hedgerows and woods will last well if the material is properly conditioned by making vertical cuts a couple of inches up woody stems and by giving everything a long drink in deep water before arranging. All wild material is hypersensitive: its life depends not only on how long it has been without water after picking, but on the composition of the water itself. Water with a high chemical content (as in urban areas) greatly reduces longevity.

This is the season for roses. Rose-growing has now become highly competitive and, with the appearance of so many new hybrids, the charm of the old-fashioned shrub roses is often overlooked: though they do not last well when cut, they are worth growing for their profusion of bloom and delicious scent. (Many modern roses are so perfectly formed that they have an artificial quality, and they are often *quite* odourless.) Floribundas are useful for picking and have an exceptionally long flowering period. Roses are always effective arranged by themselves with their own foliage, but also make excellent focal points in mixed groups. Big cabbage roses look beautiful arranged simply in a low china or silver container with their own leaves. Yellow, cream and white roses have a luminous quality that is enhanced by arranging them in a silver bowl against a background of dark antique furniture.

Since flowers are not expensive, summer is the time for large group arrangements. Foxglove, delphinium, stock, peony, *Phila-*

A simple table arrangement of white Peonies with Philadelphus set against a terracotta coloured wall.

A pair of pyramid arrangements for the mantelpiece in Lady Pulbrook's dining-room. 'Verhagen' roses, Thalictrum, Hemlock seed, Tulip Tree flowers (Lirio-dendron tulipfera), variegated Ivy, grapes and rose leaves are wired to foundations of moss and wire netting, and set in 'bronze' finished ceramic compotes.

delphus (Mock orange), canterbury bells, mixed with *Sorbus* leaves, artichoke leaves and a caladium plant makes a beautiful group on a grand scale. The same combination, using only white flowers, is infalliby beautiful for church decoration. Another popular idea for a summer wedding: large clusters of white daisies and ivy plants, which look like branches off some rare and exotic tree. (These are made by securing the plants to a base of chicken wire and moss.) Although it is hard to beat the stunning effect of all white arrangements, groups of mixed garden flowers in brilliant colours can be extremely effective.

Perhaps summer's most useful gift to the flower arranger is the peony, a sumptuous baroque flower with a rare combination of dignity and delicacy. The tree peony (*Paeonia suffruticosa*) was regarded by the ancient Chinese as 'King of flowers', a symbol of nobility, wealth and position as well as a bringer of good fortune. Apart from their splendour, these flowers are also extremely hardy, being native to China and the Himalayas: they can survive winter frost with amazing vigour, but should be started in a sheltered spot by a wall. The herbaceous species as well as the shrub varieties of peony make good focal points for compositions of mixed summer flowers. They have attractive foliage and look very handsome in simple arrangements on their own; the most lovely shades – cream, ivory, white and shell pink – have the pale, almost faded quality of antique fabrics and, compared to the more garish shades of

A large loose group in shades of yellow and white, using mixed summer flowers: Lilies, Roses, Peonies, Irises and Delphiniums.

Decorations for an early summer wedding. The pedestal vase holds a traditional group of Hydrangeas with mixed foliages and Grape and Ivy trails. The arch is decorated with a mass of Hydrangeas and Marguerites.

magenta, deep pink and yellow, they are soft and pleasantly mellow.

Resist, if you can, the temptation to cram summer vases simply because the garden offers so much choice: all the enchantment of individual details, like the silhouette of a single stem, or the translucency of a petal, is lost in a crowd. Also, beware of becoming too involved at any time with the so-called technicalities dictated largely by glossy magazines and various Do-it-yourself books. Nature has a casual harmony which can only be caught and emulated intuitively if you are not hamstrung by preconceptions of strained, finite compositions reminiscent of the provincial hairdresser's salon where hairstyles often emerge as overworked and gummy as the floral decor. Book knowledge should be only a supplement for experience, not a substitute, and is only of value when it has been assimilated; a mind choked with technical information has no room for expansion and the imagination becomes paralysed.

Large traditional mixed summer group including Rhododendron, Delphinium, Foxgloves, Agapanthus Lilies, Peonies, Rose trails and Copper beech.

A miniature mixed summer group: old fashioned Roses, perennial Pea, variegated Periwinkle, Daisies, Jasmine, Honeysuckle, Spirea, Eryngium, Heuchera, Lamb's Ears (Stachys lanata), Clematis seed-heads, and Poppy seed-heads.

A loose, disarrayed composition in shades of yellow and cream, combining Spirea, Lilies, Rose trails, Ladder Fern (Nephrolepsis exaltata), Angelica, Cornus and Copper Beech.

62

A large traditional summer arrangement including Rhododendron, Delphinium, Foxgloves, Agapanthus Lilies, Peonies, Rose trails and Copper beech.

63

An arrangement of mixed greenery on a stripped pine cabinet in the dining-room of a London apartment. Most of the material was gathered from the countryside, and includes variegated Cornus, ornamental vine, Acanthus, Hosta leaves, variegated Privet, Fennel, Foxglove seed-heads, Atriplex, *Shell Flower* (Molucella laevis), *Red-hot poker* (Kniphofia uvaria), Ballota, *Iris sheaves and seed-pods*, and variegated Ivy.

A party decoration for a buffet table in Ascot Week. *The pyramid arrangement, constructed on a base of wire mesh and moss, was made with red currants and Stephanotis, with trails of variegated Ivy, and placed on a white porcelain urn.*

Previous page

A low coffee table arrangement of Cow Parsley and meadow grasses in a simple glass beaker. Extra grass stems were used to stabilize the arrangement, rather than wire netting which is not recommended where it will be visible.

An unusual arrangement of simple material for a modern studio in Chelsea. The Italian porcelain pot holds a bouquet of Cornflowers, Love-in-a-Mist (Nigella), and Edelweiss.

A delicate arrangement for a modern studio, combining pinks, and meadow grasses in a black Spanish pottery bowl.

On the coffee table in Lady Pulbrook's drawing-room in London: 'Roselandia' roses simply and loosely arranged with Honeysuckle in a porcelain and gilt compote with tripod figure base.

Below left

A table centrepiece for a dinner party at Lady Pulbrook's house in London. 'Virgo' roses are arranged with Ivy in a low silver compote.

A mixed group of Roses arranged on an 18th century table in Lady Pulbrook's drawing-room in London. The container is a white porcelain basket. The Roses include 'Madame Butterfly', 'Lady Sylvia', 'Super Star', 'Ena Harkness', 'Virgo', 'Peace' and trails of 'Albertine'.

Bridal bouquet of Auratum Lilies. These were chosen to harmonize with the rich cream-coloured silk of the bride's dress.

Bridesmaids with a garland of yellow and pink Roses, Guelder rose (Viburnum opulus), and Pinks (Dianthus).

Previous page

An arrangement of mixed greenery suitable for a large table. The material includes Copper beech, Mahonia, Euphorbia, Guelder Rose, Iris leaves and stems, Megasea leaves, Artichoke leaves, variegated Ivy, yellow Privet, old fashioned rose trails, and a Chlorophytum plant.

A pedestal group for a wedding in a small country church. The arrangement combines Marguerites, 'Iceberg' roses, trails of pink 'New Dawn' roses, 'Peace' roses, white Delphinium, Phlox and wild Hemlock.

In the stone font of a country church, a simple loose composition of Philadelphus, 'Peace' and 'Iceberg' roses, Lady's Mantle (Alchemilla mollis) *and* Fennel (Foeniculum).

A large pedestal arrangement in cream and white for a wedding. Whitebeam sprays, Artichoke leaves and a Caladium plant form the background for Regalia Lilies, Foxgloves, Delphiniums, Peonies and Philadelphus.

77

Traditional all-white church decorations for a wedding at St. Margaret's, Westminster. Flanking the West door (above) are Daisy bushes with Ivy trails, made by fixing the plants to chicken wire bases. The ends of the pews are decorated with Marguerites, white Peonies and mixed foliage. In front of the choir stalls are two Daisy bushes, and on the altar steps two large fan-shaped arrangements of Peonies, Delphinium, Foxgloves, Philadelphus, Artichoke and Whitebeam leaves, with a Caladium plant in the centre.

Right

A free cone-shaped arrangement on a foundation of moss and wire netting placed in a cupidon vase of white pottery. Lilies, Gardenias, 'Venus' roses, and Euphorbia vulgaris combine with grapes, Berberis mahonia berries, Peperomia leaves and variegated Ivy.

An arrangement in the window of Pulbrook & Gould's shop in Sloane Street. This includes Regalia, Longiflorum *and Arum Lilies, Guelder Rose* (Viburnum opulus) *and Artichoke leaves. Below are bunches of Pinks, Lily-of-the-Valley and 'Verhagen' Roses.*

Opposite page

A large pedestal group for a drawing-room. Copper beech leaves, Philadelphus and foxgloves form a background for Peonies, Lilies, Rhododendron and Delphinium, and silvery-grey Artichoke leaves.

Mixed summer flowers and foliage in Pulbrook & Gould's shop in Sloane Street.

autumn

In Autumn the flower garden is in decline, so it is sensible to make full use of the great variety of coloured foliages and berries to be found in the countryside as well as the garden. Maple, flaming oak, horse-chestnut and beech turn to glorious shades of red, gold and brown, while shiny red, orange or black berries are scattered through the woods and hedgerows. One of the most beautiful berried trees is the rowan or mountain ash (*Sorbus aucuparis*); both

Photographed outside Pulbrook & Gould's shop in London: a mass of pink Hydrangeas with yellow single Chrysanthemums, planted in a cast iron jardinière with Ivy. These large planted arrangements are easy to maintain as well as being extremely effective.

The font of a country church, decorated for the unveiling of a memorial stained-glass window. Here 'Super Star' roses, green Hydrangeas (H. arborescens grandiflora) and spray Chrysanthemums are combined with Privet, Firethorn (Pyracantha coccinea lalandii) and trailing Ivy in a warm autumnal colour scheme. All the material used in this arrangement is ideal for church decoration, being long-lasting and easy to handle.

A pyramid arrangement for a buffet table in a white pottery compote. The material is wired on to a foundation of wire mesh and moss. The composition includes clusters of Cotoneaster berries (C. watereri), Guernsey lilies (Nerine sarniensis), 'Venus' roses, grapes, Clematis seed-heads, Peperomia leaves, berried Ivy, variegated and green Ivy leaves. Photographed in the Carole Austen salon of couture in London.

A simple arrangement of single white spray Chrysanthemums and Viburnum fragrans *in a silver compote, designed for the French Embassy in London. The table is a Louis XIV table à gibier, and behind is a 17th century Aubusson tapestry depicting* Les Portières *with the arms of France and Navarre.*

wild and cultivated varieties have magnificent clusters of scarlet or orange berries set off by feathery leaves. The cotoneaster has scarlet or black berries even in the depths of winter. The orange and yellow berries of two species of firethorn (*Pyracantha*) make excellent background material for groups of autumn flowers. The yellow berries of *Pyracantha rogersiana flava* will brighten a large composition; *P. coccinea lalandii* has bright orange berries which look rich and rare combined with cream flowers such as *Hydrangea paniculata* (which turns from cream to beige as it ripens), and gladiolus. *Lilium auratum* also has cream coloured flowers but with dark terracotta markings. Snowberry (*Symphoricarpus*) has clusters of white (deadly poisonous) berries which remain on the twigs well into winter. The evergreen and deciduous varieties of berberis also have colourful berries, red, purple or blue-black, and add lustre to dried arrangements. Especially effective with autumn flowers – particularly chrysanthemums – are the bare, arched branches of golden weeping willow and lichen-covered branches.

Pale colour schemes are in harmony with the season and pale flowers also blend with dried leaves and seed-heads. Hop flowers, cream-coloured chrysanthemums and *Lilium auratum, Hydrangea arborescens grandiflora* (whose cream heads turn a lovely shade of green when mature), the seed-heads of Old Man's Beard (*Clematis vitalba*) and the green variety of Love-lies-bleeding (*Amaranthus caudatus viridis*) all provide excellent material for compositions based

on pale colour schemes.

Combining fresh with dried material can counteract the stifling effect sometimes created by an arrangement of all dried material. It is, of course, necessary to fit a separate water container into the vase for a mixed arrangement of fresh and dried material, as the dried material will turn mouldy in water.

It is worth trying to find branches of foliage, berries and seed-heads which have good lines. In the language of painting the style of decoration inspired by this season would be called linear, as the emphasis is on expressiveness of outline in contrast to typical spring and summer arrangements, which could be called painterly, where expression relies more on the manipulation of mass, shadows and bright colours than on line. Large, sculptural arrangements of fruit (which is plentiful) and flowers are particularly effective as table centre-pieces: for instance, a pyramid of grapes, arranged

A fruit and floral trophy for the entrance hall of the Carole Austen salon of couture in Curzon Street, London. The material is wired on to a base of wire mesh and moss. The composition includes water melon, bunches of green grapes, crab-apples, aubergines, red peppers, ornamental cabbage, Scarborough Lilies (Vallota speciosa), Old Man's Beard (Clematis vitalba), Firethorn (Pyracantha coccinea lalandii), Privet with black autumn berries (Lingustrum ovalifolium aureum), Iris (I. foetidissima variegata), 'Super Star' roses, flame-coloured Dahlias, and a Croton plant (Codiaeum).

A large group in the style of a Dutch flower-piece painting, using mixed fruit, flowers and berries.

Next page

A buffet-table decoration for a party in the Tate Gallery in London. 'Super Star' roses, Cotoneaster, Old Man's Beard (Clematis vitalba), *and Ivy trails.*

A bouquet arrangement for the French Embassy in London. The white Italian pottery urn holds a fairly loose arrangement of mixed single Chrysanthemums, Lilies (Lilium longiflorum harrisii), *green Hydrangea* (H. arborescens grandiflora), *yellow Privet* (Lingustrum ovalifolium aureum), *berried Ivy, Camellia foliage and Eucalyptus.*

with gardenias or small roses makes a charming decoration for a round dining table.

A similar arrangement could be made with different coloured grapes, using leaves instead of flowers. A stemmed vase will counterbalance the bulky, pyramid shapes of these arrangements – a low bowl can look clumsy. However, make sure the centre-piece does not tower above seated guests: they may conceivably wish to see the people they are talking to. A pyramid arrangement is constructed on a base of wire mesh and moss into which the fruit, leaves and flowers are fixed by short, stiff wires attached to the stems or looped through the flesh of a fruit.

An arrangement in the form of a trophy is particularly useful in the autumn. These can be made entirely of dried materials, or a combination of dried and fresh. Gourds, seed-heads, cones and leaves, all previously dried or preserved, combine well with fresh fruit, vegetables and berries; fresh material is best placed in an accessible position, as it may need replacing. Artichokes are particularly good material for this type of arrangement: not only do they have extremely decorative shapes and colours, but also the advantage of drying out rather than rotting in an arrangement when they have been used fresh. Again, for construction, an a base of wire mesh camouflaged with moss is used, while the fruits, leaves, seed-heads, cones, etc. are attached with shortish stiff wires. Sprayed gold or silver they make elegant Christmas

decorations, especially if combined with swags of fresh evergreens.

The autumn crocus (*Colchicum*) is among the most charming of autumn flowers. Surprisingly enough, these delicate looking flowers last well when cut. They look best arranged on their own, perhaps in a miniature silver container; a kenzan, or pinholder, is the best method of fixing their very fragile stems. The winter daffodil (*Sternbergia lutea*) – a bulbous plant with yellow, crocus-like flowers – though rather difficult to grow, can be used for a charming planted dish with moss, ivy, *Viburnum fragrans*, a few freesias and any other small flowers which are available. Bear in mind that small flowers look best in planted dishes, as they are more in scale with the 'landscape' and create the illusion of a miniature garden.

For autumn weddings a cream-toned colour scheme makes an agreeable change. Yucca lilies, gardenias, stephanotis on its own branches, are all good material for a bride's bouquet. Combina-

A buffet-table decoration for the French Embassy in London. The large mass bouquet of autumn material is arranged in a white pottery urn. It is composed of a mixture of large single Chrysanthemums and sprays of single Chrysanthemums in white and pastel shades, with yellow and red Cotoneaster and Hydrangea. The foliage is Privet and Eucalyptus, berried Ivy, and trails of green Ivy.

Opposite page
A large party bouquet arrangement for a reception at the French Embassy in London. The vast high-ceilinged rooms are exquisitely furnished with French antique pieces and tapestries, so an arrangement which was bold, formal, but subdued in colour was required.

tions of pale-coloured flowers make beautiful church decorations, perhaps mixed with coloured foliages and berries. Colour schemes of a redder tone are also within the scope of seasonal material. For instance, stems of dark pink hydrangeas, the brilliantly coloured foliage of *Hydrangea quercifolia*, dahlias, roses and the hybrid *Sedum* 'Autumn Joy' or *Sedum maximum atropurpureum* are all eminently suited to this kind of decoration.

Scales used as hanging baskets in an interior. The unusual mixture of fruit and flowers combines Dahlias, Nerine Lilies, Cotoneaster, Old Man's Beard (Clematis vitalba), Caladium leaves and grapes.

Left

A traditional sideboard or buffet decoration. The tall silver épergne holds grapes, oranges, apples, pears, bananas and lemons, with Chlorophytum plants and Ivy. This type of arrangement, dismissed so briskly by Mrs Beeton as rather ordinary, is so rarely seen nowadays that it has a special charm. The materials are quite inexpensive.

Next page

A trophy decoration for Robert Carrier's restaurant in Camden Passage, London. This piece is made of bread, skeleton and preserved magnolia leaves, and barley.

winter

A large pedestal group for a wedding reception in London.

A planted dish for Robert Carrier's restaurant in Camden Passage, London. The all-green tones look cool and refreshing against the whitewashed brick wall.

The winter months could be quite the most boring and frustrating for any would-be flower arranger were it not for the existence of dried material, and the increasing range of fresh flowers shipped from overseas, and grown in the hothouse at home. One's choice of material should be guided by what is in season. An arrangement composed of material that is ostentatiously incongruous can be rather vulgar.

A pyramid arrangement of artificial fruit combined with dried and preserved seed-heads, ferns and grasses, sprayed with gold paint for Christmas decoration in Robert Carrier's restaurant. The brassy-gold finish combines well with the strong colouring of the green baize wall covering, scarlet table-cloths, black painted furniture and brass lampshades.

Evergreens are an obvious standby, as are any flowers which are grown relatively easily in a hothouse. Some flowers, particularly chrysanthemums, poinsettias, guelder roses and certain lilies, have a seasonal association. The best winter foliages are the hardy evergreens such as *Camellia japonica*, whose unusual shiny leaves mix well with other evergreens or, on their own, make a simple background for a few sprays of flowers. Also useful are two species of *Prunus*: Portugal laurel (*P. lusitanica*) and cherry laurel (*P. laurocerasus*). Both of these have well-shaped shiny green leaves, and are slightly cheaper than camellia branches. For a silvery-grey background it is easy to find eucalyptus (an Australian gum) in two imported varieties: *E. populifolius*, having round leaves, and *E. globulus* with pointed ones. Both last well. *E. gunnii* is another species which grows in Britain. Also good for grey backgrounds is the blue cedar (*Cedrus atlantica glauca*) which has gracefully shaped branches and magnificent cones. Its gun-metal colour is beautifully

A pyramid arrangement for Carrier's Restaurant made of potted plants: Chlorophytum, Cryptanthus, Tradescantia, Croton, and Ivies.

offset by eucalyptus and a few single chrysanthemums. Other useful background materials are holly, variegated holly, larch, spruce, pine, trails of ivy, plain or berried, and lichen covered branches.

As explained in the chapter on dried material, some of these foliages can be dried after they have been used fresh. Laurel and eucalyptus are both suited to glycerine treatment. Blue cedar branches should be hung until they are thoroughly dried and all the needles have been shed. The bare branches have clean, sweeping shapes which can be sprinkled with Christmas glitter or sprayed gold or silver.

The chrysanthemum is the backbone of winter flower arrangement. It is a greenhouse plant, a hardy and half-hardy perennial, and on the whole quite cheap. There are many species of chrysanthemum, differing in colour and shape, and all last outstandingly well when cut, longer perhaps than any other flower. The varieties of single chrysanthemum, such as the Korean, are particularly graceful and pretty: a few sprays arranged with foliage can be most effective. On the whole the single chrysanthemum is the best; it has interesting and clearly delineated shapes, whereas the double varieties are more massive and blob-like and tend to make an arrangement look pompous, if they are not used with great discretion. Chrysanthemums are also satisfactory as house plants. Their close and long-standing association with Chinese art and flower arrangement means that they will look right in a Chinese

A small ornamental tree made from dried Ruscus leaves wired to a base of wire mesh and moss, sprayed with gold paint. The trunk and base of the tree are made of alabastine modelled on a wire framework. Plastic 'pearls' have been attached to the branches. These little trees are effective among antiques and objets, such as the 17th century Italian brass lion in the illustration, and make a pleasant contrast to traditional Christmas decorations. (See also p.112.)

A traditional decoration for a Christmas party in London. The decoration was designed to enhance the formal 18th century style of this large reception room. Poinsettias (Euphorbia pulcherrima) and pink Azaleas are surrounded by sprays of pine, holly and lichen-covered twigs.

vase amongst eighteenth century furniture and *chinoiseries*. Needless to say, they look just as good in modern settings.

Any available variety of viburnum is attractive in winter arrangements. *V. fragrans* has a delicious scent and pretty white and pink flowers. The guelder rose (*V. opulus*) has round flowers and beautiful foliage: the flower is particularly effective while still a greenish colour as it then has a luminescence quite unlike any other colour.

The guelder rose, with chrysanthemums, carnations and tulips (also available at this time of year) was greatly favoured by Dutch flower-piece painters. It is well worth looking at these still-lifes as a source of inspiration for winter arrangements: the style is easy to emulate, even if you cannot find the exact material.

Another useful winter flower is *Euphorbia*: poinsettia (*E. pulcherrima*) appears before Christmas, and *E. fulgens* comes into the

A candlestick decorated for a Christmas party with a small wreath of pine, variegated holly and red carnations wired around the base.

An entrance hall decorated for a Christmas dance in a London house. Twisted round the pillars are trails of pine and ivy wired together and decorated with silvered pine cones and tiny blue lights. The tree is hung with silvered wire cobwebs, blue silvered glass balls, silvered pine cones, glass icicles, and artificial Christmas roses. A two-colour scheme for large-scale Christmas decoration – as illustrated here – can be far more effective than a multi-coloured one.

shops in January. Both are expensive hothouse varieties; they should not be cut, but used potted or with their roots washed. The former has brilliant red or white flowers and well shaped leaves, the latter curved sprays of orange flowers. A third variety (now being imported to Britain from America) is called *Euphorbia robbiae*. It has evergreen foliage and is not a hothouse plant. Poinsettias look particularly beautiful mixed with azaleas, holly and other evergreens.

Winter weddings present something of a problem. The traditional pedestal vases require long-stemmed flowers which must be imported and can be prohibitively expensive. A simple green and white colour scheme would be attractive and appropriate: for instance, white lilac (from the South of France) mixed with lilies and catkins, against a background of rhododendron leaves. White poinsettias look as magnificent as they are expensive. White azalea plants provide good focal points in large arrangements but, again,

The fireplace of a London night-club decorated for a Christmas dance. A carved wooden eagle perches on a nest of lichen-covered twigs, Poinsettias (Euphorbia pulcherrima), variegated holly, spruce, pine cones and driftwood.

A candelabrum decorated for a Christmas dinner party with a bouquet of spruce, variegated holly, red carnations and sprigs of Winter Jasmine (Jasminum nudiflorum).

A small table arrangement of 'Chiffon' roses, Freesias, Eucalyptus (E. globulus) and variegated Ivy, arranged in a white porcelain mermaid vase. This essentially feminine arrangement is a classical boudoir bouquet in the Pompadour tradition.

A tree made of artificial leaves and berries fastened to a trunk of alabastine on a wire base, sprayed gold and dusted with 'glitter'.

are depressingly expensive at this time of year.

For table decoration, fruit, flower and foliage combinations are always successful: for instance a small pyramid of green grapes with roses, built up on a base of wire and moss, with a few leaves. On the sideboard a grander effect can be achieved using an epergne of fruit with ivy trails and Chlorophytum.

Long-lasting decorations can be made by planting dishes of hyacinths, snowdrops, crocuses and polyanthus, set off by moss and ivy; or by arranging bowls of mixed greenhouse plants such as ivy, small ferns and Tradescantia. T. fluminensis has green and white leaves which become tinged with pink if exposed to sunlight. It adds character to small vases of cut flowers and is suitable for bouquets and planted dishes. The hardy flowering variety, T. virginiana (Moses in the Bulrushes), has a three-petalled flower which, in blue, white and mauve, is a good mixer.

An ornamental tree made of skeleton
Magnolia leaves dyed red and wired to a
base of alabastine on a wire frame. The
tree has been sprayed with gold paint and
decorated with silver glass balls and
'glitter'.

A drawing-room or sideboard group for
Christmas. An old copper cooking kettle
holds silvered Birch and Pine twigs,
variegated holly, fir cones, artificial poinsettias and silvered wire spider webs.

Next page

Artificial trees for Christmas decoration.

Entrance hall decoration in a London apartment. The loose, arching bouquet combines 'Verhagen' roses, Chlorophytum, green Hellebore (Helleborus viridis), Dracaena (D. fragans victoriae), Peperomia (P. magnifolia), Euphorbia fulgens and Ivy trails.

A Christmas decoration for the sideboard or a niche. The white pottery head vase is laden with sprigs of spruce, silver painted artificial fruit, artificial Christmas roses, and skeleton Magnolia leaves. Pink candles and ribbon complete this extravagant head-dress.

A planted dish for the drawing-room of a
modern apartment in London. The colours
were chosen to blend with the colours of the
picture behind and the ancient horse found in
China. Planted in a flat pottery dish are
Begonia rex, Sedum, Tradescantia,
and African Violets with driftwood and
moss.

appendix:

Over 20 years ago, Susan Pulbrook and Rosamund Gould rented a basement in Halkin Street, London, S.W.1, to turn into a florists' workshop. The idea of the partnership was experimental. Lady Pulbrook, whose husband had just died, was deeply depressed and in need of a therapeutic occupation. She had always loved working with flowers and, although untrained, was lucky to have 'green fingers' and a natural flair for flower arrangement. Miss Gould, who had trained as a professional florist at the Constance Spry School, was freelancing but had reached a point at which her orders threatened to swamp her and she needed an extra hand to cope.

From the start, finding sources of fresh material was a major concern. They made frequent excursions into the country to pick flowers and foliage, and the buying trip to Covent Garden became a regular early morning event. They drove their own van, wheeled their own barrow of purchased goods, arranged the flowers and delivered the orders. A year later, they moved to their present Sloane Street shop and took on a staff of two.

Business continued to increase and the scale of their commissions expanded, demanding a greater variety of stock to meet sophisticated requests. Moving from their relatively quiet basement to Sloane Street brought them into direct contact with the public; carrying on with work while frequently interrupted by visiting shoppers, was just one of the early difficulties they had to face. Both of them were still learning, certainly the business side, and since perfecting the art of flower arrangement only ceases with interest in the subject, they were apprentices on both scores.

A significant turning point in their career was a commission to decorate a large, dreary hotel basement for a debutante dance. They decided to disguise it as a formal 17th century garden, complete with elaborate topiary hedging and a fountain. All the material was prepared in Lady Pulbrook's back garden in London and, with Miss Gould's help, transported to the site and assembled like a pre-fabricated house. The result was voted a terrific success on the night – the clients were delighted. Word spread and commissions snowballed. This particular project was valuable for the confidence and experience it gave and, ever since, large-scale decorations have been a speciality.

Satisfied that their teamwork could continue, creative and profitable, Lady Pulbrook and Miss Gould laid definite plans for the future. Determined to have a constant source of fresh flowers and foliage, they established contacts outside London with owners of private estates who agreed to grow special orders for them. The variety of unusual flowers, grasses and mosses, etc. thus provided kept the shop diversely stocked and, being used in their flower arrangement, helped to establish their reputation for exceptional quality, variety and originality.

Professional flower buyers in London needed to know Covent Garden's geographical layout backwards, to say nothing of its psychological structure. Fortunately for Pulbrook & Gould, they managed to combine a working knowledge of horticulture with the necessary bargaining power even in the small hours of the morning.

Pulbrook & Gould's views on flower arrangement can be summed up quite simply. Like most contemporary flower arrangers, they owe much to Constance Spry's example. They hate, as she did, formal, tightly-composed arrangements. Instead, they aim at loose, fresh and natural compositions. As a 'painting', an arrangement has to grow from the inspiration of its creator. Size is determined by the setting but the creative urge is unpredictable: the shape of each piece helps to determine the overall design and the relation of colours produces an illusion of depth. Like painters, florists often overwork their creation in the final stages and risk destroying its initial spontaneity. The danger is to use up material at hand just because it happens to be left over; knowing just when to stop is a knack learned only by experience and self-discipline.

Training is not vital to the making of a flower arranger but technical knowledge will help amateurs to handle the paraphernalia of an arrangement with dexterity, speed, efficiency and confidence. The chances of flowers becoming damaged are minimal in hands that are disciplined and accustomed to working with the equipment. Pulbrook & Gould run day and evening classes, mostly for housewives, in which they teach them the basic techniques: how to manipulate wire netting, for instance, or how to condition various kinds of material to make it last. Their full-scale training course is much more comprehensive. School leavers are taken on as apprentices and learn the craft in the shop, the workrooms or on locations with senior decorators.

The professional flower decorator works long hours and often in nerve-racking conditions. Flowers for weddings, receptions and so on, have to be left till the last minute, so the arranger must be prepared to work quietly and independently of surrounding caterers, harassed decorators and over-excited hostesses. The material is messy and fragile. Long green branches, cartons of fruit, potted plants, all tend to drip, shred or crumble in the midst of crisply-laundered, white damask table-cloths, immaculately polished silver and glass, pale pristine carpets and priceless antiques. Working against time, the florist has to move with the precision of a cat, make decisions with a financier's speed and possess a diplomat's tact. Imagination is, naturally, an asset, but quite useless unless it is matched by nerves of steel and practical skill. The exacting task of the professional florist makes the conventions of Ikenobo sound quite sensible. The element of calm, which should be fundamental to the entire operation, is also appropriate to the Western situation and, as Ikenobo maintains, flower arrangments do indeed reflect the mood of the arranger.